I AM
Challenge

MELODY A OLSON

I AM CHALLENGE

ISBN: 978-0-9909039-4-9

DEDICATION

To my Jeff.
Thank you for letting me be me until I found
out who me really was.
I LOVE YOU.

ACKNOWLEDGMENTS

I give first credits to my time in the prayer closet. It was in this sacred place that I found me, huddled many nights in tears as the line between the truth and believing it became thinner. I am thankful the Lord is relentless in His pursuit of us. On this side of Heaven I want to acknowledge my tribe of warriors who stood alongside me on the front line as I fought this battle to shed the shroud of guilt, shame and condemnation to come to the place where I understood the truth of who I am, because I understand who He is.

1
WHAT IS THE I AM CHALLENGE?

The words we speak have power. The I AM Challenge was birthed out of my prayer closet after time of fasting and prayer; a time of absolute silence.

During this time I came to the realization of the words I had spoken over my life had to be undone and re-spun.

God brought a revelation...which is now my purpose: to teach others to Speak Life & Live!

This 21 day journey is truly life giving and if you will accept the challenge, it can lead you to create a habit to Speak Life & Live for yourself and those around you - Be careful - it's contagious.

Since 2011 hundreds have taken the I AM Challenge and we expect it to grow even bigger.

When we hear our own voice speak - faith and belief connect! This has become a foundational principle of Speak Life & Live.

So then faith comes by hearing, and hearing by the word of God.

Romans 10:17 (NKJV)

HOW DO I START?

Each day for the next 21 Days you will receive the I AM Statement of the day:

The challenge is threefold: READ. POST. SHARE.

- Read your I AM statement and scripture aloud to yourself a minimum of 10 times throughout the day.

- Post your I AM statement and scripture on your social media via Facebook/Twitter/Instagram/YouTube/Periscope, etc.

- Share your I AM statement and scripture to at least one other person face to face each day.

The place to begin is right away in the morning, in front of the mirror and then again, as many times as you can throughout your day.

The goal is to Speak Life & Live.

Remember when we hear our own voice speak - faith and belief connect.

Think of it as a "Fitbit" for your mouth - the more times you say it - the more the I AM will become a part of you.

When you finish this challenge you will Speak Life & Live.

By days end the words you have spoken over yourself will become part of you, ingrained because you have chosen to speak life and live over yourself.

The next part of the challenge is to Post online and Share in a conversation.

Join the I AM Challenge facebook page: https://www.facebook.com/21dayiAMchall enge/

Speak Life & Live!

When we hear our own voice proclaim the Word of God, our mind, body and soul own it.

Faith comes by hearing, and hearing by the word of God. Romans 10:17

I am personally praying for you to experience a transformation in understanding who you are and whose you are as you speak life with each I AM of the day, that it will encourage you in seeking your true identity in Christ.

If you take this challenge seriously, you will never be the same again.

Let the words of my mouth and the meditation of my heart be acceptable in thy sight of the Lord. Psalm 19:14.

It's your time to begin to reclaim who you were created to be...

I AM CHALLENGE

I AM

CHALLENGE

READ.POST. SHARE

DAY 1

I AM

Chosen

Even before the world was made,
God had already chosen me to be his through
my union with Christ,
so that I would be holy and without fault
before him.
Because of His love
Ephesians 1:4 (GNT)

NOTES

READ. POST. SHARE.

DAY 2

I AM

Led by the Holy Spirit

For I speak as a messenger approved by God
to be entrusted with the Good News.
My purpose is to please God, not people.
He alone examines the motives of my heart.
1 Thessalonians 2:4

NOTES

READ. POST. SHARE.

DAY 3

I AM

a Child of God

And now that I belong to Christ,
I AM the true child of Abraham.
I AM his heir, and God's promise to
Abraham belongs to me.
Galations 3:29

NOTES

READ. POST. SHARE.

DAY 4

I AM

Set Apart

"God knew me BEFORE He formed me in
your mother's womb.
BEFORE I was born, He set me apart
and appointed me as His prophet to the
nations."
Jeremiah 1:5 NLT

NOTES

READ. POST. SHARE.

DAY 5

I AM

a New Creation

I AM a new creature in Christ.
2 Corinthians 5:17

NOTES

READ. POST. SHARE.

DAY 6

I AM

Redeemed

Yet God, with undeserved kindness,
declares that I AM righteous.
He did this through Christ Jesus when he
freed me from the
penalty for my sins.
Romans 3:24

NOTES

READ. POST. SHARE.

DAY 7

I AM

Invited

In him and through faith in him
I may approach God with freedom and
confidence.
Ephesians 3:12

NOTES

READ. POST. SHARE.

DAY 8

I AM

Worthy

And God will wipe every tear from my
face.
He'll remove signs of disgrace from me,
wherever I AM.
YES! God says so!
Isaiah 25:8

NOTES

READ. POST. SHARE.

DAY 9

I AM

His Favorite

God delights in the well-being of me, His
servant.
Psalm 35:27

NOTES

READ. POST. SHARE.

DAY 10

I AM

Obediently Blessed

God will defeat my enemies who attack me.
Deuteronomy 28:7-14

NOTES

READ. POST. SHARE.

BONUS!

Congratulations! You are halfway through.

Can you feel the shift in your heart and mind?

That's called Belief!

Love speaks louder than any
other language. ~M

If you must talk - Speak Life.
~M

Speaking life begins with thinking life. If our thoughts are not for life, than our words can't be. ~M

Do you understand your worth? Oh!! If you could only begin to grasp the reality of how magnificent you are. ~M

It's not about being perfect...it's about perfecting our faith to align with our words. ~M

If I feel the need to speak my mind, I stop and speak my heart instead. ~M

God Gave His Word

13-18 When God made his promise to Abraham, he backed it to the hilt, putting his own reputation on the line. He said, "I promise that I'll bless you with everything I have—bless and bless and bless!" Abraham stuck it out and got everything that had been promised to him. When people make promises, they guarantee them by appeal to some authority above them so that if there is any question that they'll make good on the promise, the authority will back them up. When God wanted to guarantee his promises, he gave his word, a rock-solid guarantee—God can't break his word. And because his word cannot change, the promise is likewise unchangeable.

18-20 We who have run for our very lives to God have every reason to grab the promised hope with both hands and never let go. It's an unbreakable spiritual lifeline, reaching past all appearances right to the very presence of God where Jesus, running on ahead of us, has taken up his permanent post as high priest for us, in the order of Melchizedek.

Hebrews 6:13-20 MSG

12 Blessed [happy, spiritually prosperous, favored by God] is the man who is steadfast under trial and perseveres when tempted; for when he has passed the test and been approved, he will receive the [victor's] crown of life which the Lord has promised to those who love Him.

James 1:12Amplified Bible (AMP)

9 Let us not grow weary or become discouraged in doing good, for at the proper time we will reap, if we do not give in.

Galatians 6:9Amplified Bible (AMP)

DAY 11

I AM

Beautiful

I look to him and I am radiant,
my face shall never be ashamed.
Psalms 34:5

NOTES

READ. POST. SHARE.

DAY 12

I AM

Strong

I wait upon the Lord
and shall renew my strength;
I will mount up with wings as an eagle;
I will run and not be weary;
and I will walk, and not faint.
Isaiah 40:31

NOTES

READ. POST. SHARE.

DAY 13

I AM

an Overcomer

I AM an overcomer
by the blood of the Lamb
and by the word of my testimony,
I AM not afraid to die.
Revelation 12:11

NOTES

_____
_____
_____
_____
_____
_____
_____
_____
_____
_____
_____
_____
_____
_____
_____
_____
_____
_____
_____
_____
_____
_____
_____
_____
_____

READ. POST. SHARE.

DAY 14

I AM

Saved by Grace

But my life is worth nothing to me unless I use it for finishing the work assigned me by the Lord Jesus — the work of telling others the Good News about the wonderful grace of God.
Acts 20:24

NOTES

READ. POST. SHARE.

DAY 15

I AM

Loved

I know what real love is
because Jesus gave up his life for me.
1 John 3:16

NOTES

READ. POST. SHARE.

DAY 16

I AM

Forgiven

Therefore if I AM in Christ I am
a new creation 'the old is gone' the new is
here.
2 Corinthians 5:17

NOTES

READ. POST. SHARE.

DAY 17

I AM

Compassionate

I AM kind, tenderhearted, forgiving others,
as God in Christ forgave me.
Ephesians 4:32

NOTES

READ. POST. SHARE.

DAY 18

I AM

Healed and Whole

I AM healed by His stripes.
Isaiah 53:4

NOTES

READ. POST. SHARE.

DAY 19

I AM

a Warrior

Announce this to the godless nations:
Prepare for battle!
Soldiers at attention!
Present arms! Advance!
Turn your shovels into swords,
turn your hoes into spears.
Let the weak one throw out his chest
and say, "I AM tough, I AM a fighter."
Joel 3:9-10

NOTES

READ. POST. SHARE.

DAY 20

I AM

Authentic

And in Christ I AM brought to fullness.
He is the head over every power and authority.
Colossians 2:10

NOTES

READ. POST. SHARE.

DAY 21

I AM

Who He says I am

Yet in all these things, I AM more than a
conqueror and gain an overwhelming victory
through Him, who loved me!
Romans 8:37

NOTES

_____
_____
_____
_____
_____
_____
_____
_____
_____
_____
_____
_____
_____
_____
_____
_____
_____
_____
_____
_____
_____
_____
_____
_____
_____
_____
_____
_____

READ. POST. SHARE.

YOU MADE IT!

I pray this journey, though simple, was life changing for you.

As you stayed faithful to the challenge, I hope you grasped the concept that speaking life doesn't need to be complicated. It must be intentional.

Now the real challenge begins...

Speaking Life every day!

The I AM Challenge is only the beginning of the many more promises that are written in the Word for you, believing they are true is up to you.

I would love to hear how this challenge has impacted you.

Be blessed beyond measure, you are worthy of all he has to offer you. You are His favorite.

~Melody

ABOUT THE AUTHOR

Melody A. Olson founder of Speak Life & Live, is an intercessor, a writer and a storyteller with a passion to encourage others to live a life of freedom and grace. Melody and her husband are recent empty nesters, enjoying their new found solitude, living in an authentic Log Cabin in the Woods, just west of the Twin Cities in Minnesota.

Melody has a passion to encourage, uplift and empower people of all ages to grasp the understanding of how amazing life can be when we learn to speak life and live authentically! Whether she is sharing with a friend one-on-one over coffee, posting to Facebook or Twitter, writing on her blog or speaking from the stage; simply encouraging others is what she is meant to do.

Melody's mission is to help others find their true identity; she believes sharing her unique experience and speaking life into others can be the key to give them the courage to unlock answers, reveal purpose and begin their own journey to become who they were created to be…to Speak Life & Live!

Invite Melody to speak at
your next event!
www.melodyaolson.com

www.ingramcontent.com/pod-product-compliance
Lightning Source LLC
Chambersburg PA
CBHW060426050426
42449CB00009B/2160